KU-093-407

Rocks and Minerals

Keith Lye

W
FRANKLIN WATTS
LONDON•SYDNEY

This edition 2003

Franklin Watts
96 Leonard Street
London EC2A 4XD

Franklin Watts Australia
45-51 Huntley Street
Alexandria
NSW 2015

Copyright © 1992 Franklin Watts

Series editor: A. Patricia Sechi
Design: Shaun Barlow
Artwork: Michael Lye
Picture research: Ambreen Husain
Educational advisor:
Joy Richardson

A CIP catalogue record for
this book is available from the
British Library

ISBN 0 7496 5059 1

Printed in Italy

Contents

What are rocks?

Rocks are the hard parts of the **earth**. They form the earth's covering, called the **crust**. Soil and plants cover most rocks. Soil is made of worn bits of rock such as sand, **clay** and the remains of plants and animals. Rocks have many uses. Some are used in buildings. Others contain valuable metals and **minerals**.

▽ Soil and plants cover most rocks. But we can see rocks in cliffs or road cuttings.

How are rocks formed?

Under the earth's crust it is so hot that some rocks melt. The melted rock is called **magma**. Some of it comes to the surface through mountains called **volcanoes**. When magma reaches the surface, it is called lava. The lava cools and hardens to form rock. These rocks are called igneous rocks. Basalt is a common rock made from lava.

▷ The rocks at Giant's Causeway in Northern Ireland are made of basalt.

▽ Volcanic bombs are lumps of lava. They are hurled out of volcanoes.

▽ Pumice is a volcanic rock which has lots of holes.

△ Obsidian is a glassy rock. It is made from lava that has cooled quickly.

What is granite?

Granite is a rock made from magma. The magma cools and hardens below the surface of the earth. Granite is the most common rock made like this. It only appears on the surface after the rocks above it have been worn away. This happens in many mountain areas. Granite may be white, grey, pink or red.

◁ Sheets of polished granite can be used to face buildings and walls.

◁ Granite is hard rock. It is often used for kerbstones.

◁ Granite is used for sculptures. The granite is polished when the sculpture is finished.

▽ Granite often forms large parts of mountain areas.

Sedimentary rocks

Many rocks are made from bits of other rocks which have been worn away. These bits are called sediments. Rivers wash them into the sea. On the sea-bed the loose sediments are squeezed together. After a very long time they become solid rocks. Rocks formed in this way are called sedimentary rocks.

▷ Sedimentary rocks usually form in flat layers like a pile of sandwiches.

▽ Conglomerates are rocks made of pebbles set in fine sand or mud.

▷ Sandstone is made from grains of sand.

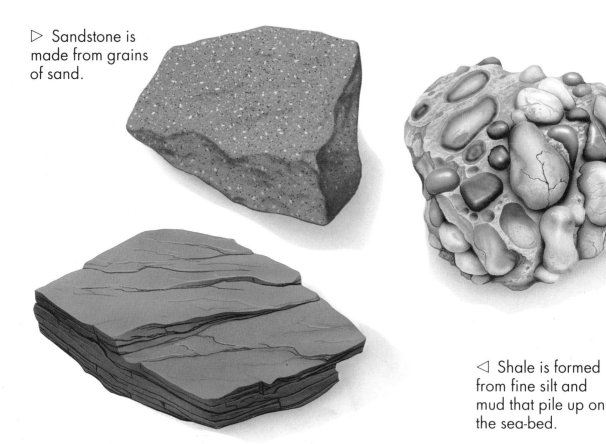

◁ Shale is formed from fine silt and mud that pile up on the sea-bed.

Fossils in rocks

Animal and plant remains are sometimes buried in sand or mud. When the sand and mud turn into hard rock, these remains may be saved as fossils. Some rocks called limestone are made up of fossils such as seashells. Chalk is a kind of limestone. It is made from the remains of animals and plants.

▽ Miners dig coal from the ground.

▷ Marks made by leaves can be found as fossils in rocks.

▽ Ammonites are ancient sea creatures. Their shells are often found as fossils.

▽ In some limestone rocks the remains of shells are clearly seen.

△ This limestone contains many small fossils.

▷ Coal is made of the remains of ancient plants which have been pressed into hard rock.

'Cooked' rocks

When you put wet dough in the oven it does not look like a loaf of bread. Heat and pressure change the dough and they change rocks too. Shale is a rock made from clay. When it is heated and squeezed it turns into a hard rock called slate. Rocks which have been changed in this way are called metamorphic rocks.

▷ Marble is cut out of the earth at quarries like this one.

▽ This piece of migmatite shows the patterns of the rock as it melted.

▽ Slate is hard rock formed from soft rock shale.

◁ Marble is formed when limestone is heated and pressed inside the earth.

What are rocks made of?

Rocks are made of minerals. Some rocks are made of only one mineral. Most rocks are made of more than one kind of mineral. Limestone rocks are made mostly of the mineral calcite. Granite often contains three minerals. These are a pink or grey feldspar, a glassy quartz and a black mineral called mica.

▽ Chalk is a white limestone. Cliffs of chalk are made up mainly of the mineral calcite.

◁ The shiny glassy substance in granite is the mineral quartz.

▽ Feldspar is a main mineral in granite. It may be pink or grey.

▷ Mica is a dark mineral often found in granite.

15

Hard and soft minerals

Diamonds are minerals. A diamond is the hardest of all natural things and it is used for cutting glass. Other minerals such as quartz are also very hard. Some minerals are very soft. Talc is a mineral used to make talcum powder. It is so soft that you can crush it with your fingernail. The hardness of minerals helps us to tell one from another.

▷ Diamonds can be used to cut patterns in glass.

▽ You can scratch the mineral calcite with a copper coin.

△ The mineral talc is soft. You can scratch it with your finger.

▽ The hardest natural substance is diamond. It is used to cut other hard materials.

▽ A special steel file is needed to scratch quartz.

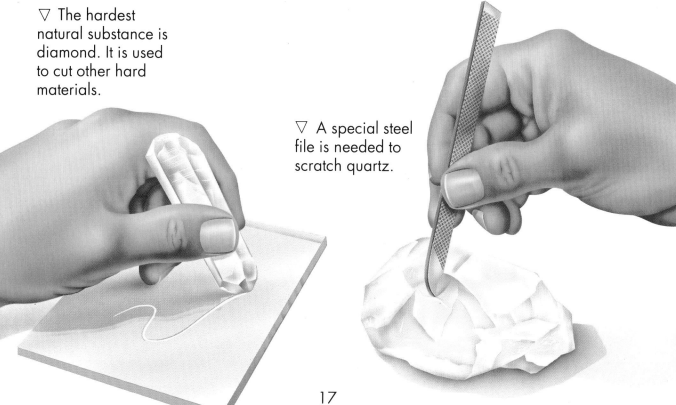

17

Crystals

If you leave a saucer of seawater in the sun, the water slowly disappears. Look through a magnifying glass and you will see that minerals in the water have formed a crust of tiny salt **crystals**. Most minerals form crystals. Crystals of the same mineral may be very different in size.

▽ Quartz forms regular-shaped crystals with flat sides.

▽ Gypsum is a mineral used to make plaster of Paris which is used to set broken bones.

△ Sulphur occurs as crystals and also as earthy masses.

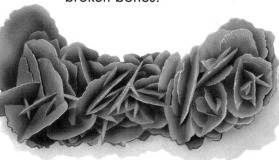

▷ Ameythst is a purple quartz. It often forms beautiful clusters of crystals.

▷ Diamond crystals usually have eight faces or sides.

▽ Zircon crystals are sometimes polished and used as jewels.

▽ Crystals of galena, a mineral which contains the metal lead.

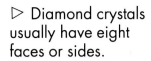

Minerals and metals

Some minerals contain useful metals. These minerals are called **ores.** We can get iron from an ore called hematite. Iron is used to make steel. Ores like these are dug out of the ground by miners. To obtain the metal the ores are crushed or heated. Metal can be used to make all sorts of objects such as cars, pipes and cans.

▽ Miners dig up metal ores from the ground.

◁ Chalcopyrite is an ore containing copper. This is used to make pipes and saucepans.

▷ Bauxite is an ore containing aluminium. This is a metal used to make cans.

◁ Hematite is an ore containing iron. Steel objects are made from iron.

Using rocks and minerals

If you crush some coloured rocks and minerals you produce powders that can be used to make paints. People once crushed the mineral hematite to produce a reddish-brown powder to make rouge.

Jewels such as rubies are used in clockwork watches. Diamonds are used to make cutting instruments. Some are used by doctors for delicate operations.

▷ Hard minerals such as rubies are used in clockwork watches.

▷ Cinnabar was used to make vermilion, a bright red paint.

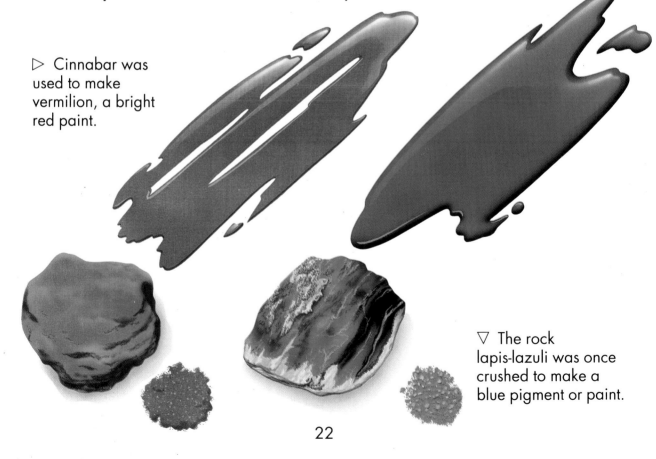

▽ The rock lapis-lazuli was once crushed to make a blue pigment or paint.

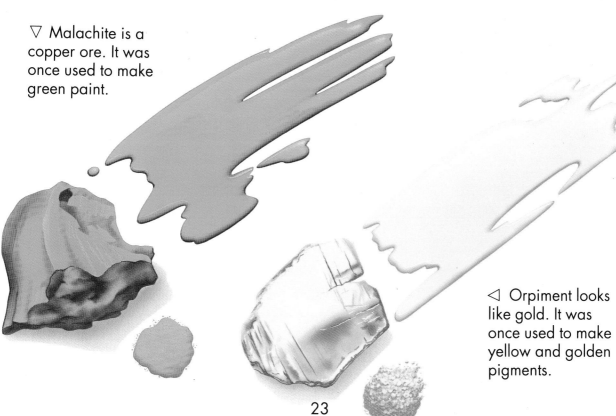

▽ Malachite is a copper ore. It was once used to make green paint.

◁ Orpiment looks like gold. It was once used to make yellow and golden pigments.

23

Valuable metals

Some metals such as gold, silver and platinum are very valuable. And they are attractive to look at. Gold, silver and platinum are rare as they are usually only found in small amounts. For hundreds of years gold and silver have been used for jewellery and coins. They are also used in industry and by dentists and doctors.

▷ Gold is sometimes used by dentists for capping teeth and also for fillings.

▷ Gold crystals are very rare. Gold is more often found as lumps called nuggets.

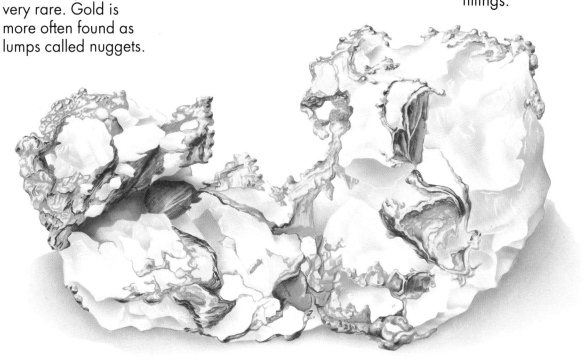

▽ Gold and silver have been used in jewellery since ancient times.

Precious stones

Some minerals called **precious stones** are used in jewellery. Diamonds are precious stones. When they are cut and polished they have a brilliant sparkle. Some diamonds may not have any colour but many are yellowish. Other precious stones are rubies which are red and sapphires which are blue.

▷ Precious stones are used to decorate jewellery and other valuable objects.

▽ Glittering stones such as diamonds are used in many kinds of jewellery.

▷ Ruby is a rare, red form of a common mineral called corundum.

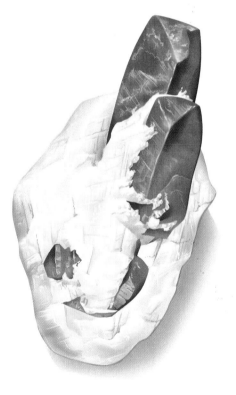

▽ Emerald is a bright green form of a mineral called beryl.

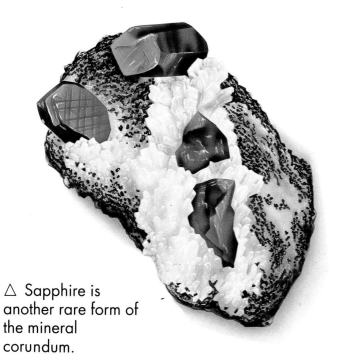

△ Sapphire is another rare form of the mineral corundum.

Other stones

There are many other beautiful minerals which may be made into jewellery. These include agate which is a striped stone, red carnelian, garnets, opal, tiger's eye and turquoise. Some of them are prized because of their colours which may change shade within one piece. Some minerals are large or tough enough to carve.

▷ Jewellers take great care in cutting and polishing stones.

▽ Garnets are found in metamorphic rocks. They occur in many colours.

▷ Agate is a mineral which has a striped pattern.

▷ Turquoise also gives its name to a blue-green colour.

△ Opal is a mineral that shows rainbow colours when you turn it around.

Things to do

- Many people collect rocks and minerals. When you visit the seashore look at the pebbles on the beach. See if you can recognize any of the rocks and minerals.

- Visit your local museum. You can find out there what common rocks and minerals are found near your home.

- Fossil collecting is also fun. On the seashore look carefully at rocks near cliffs. They often contain fossils. But never climb cliffs. The rocks are often loose and very dangerous.

Useful Addresses/Websites:

Geological Museum
Exhibition Road
London
SW7 2DE
www.nhm.ac.uk

British Geological Survey
Kingsley Dunham Centre
Keyworth
Nottingham
NG12 5GG
www.bgs.ac.uk

Glossary

aluminium A lightweight metal used for many things such as drinks cans and aeroplanes.

clay A fine substance found in most soils.

crust The outer hard shell of the earth.

crystal A crystal is a substance which forms with regular flat surfaces. Diamonds and sulphur both form as crystals.

earth The planet on which we live. Earth is also the name for the soil which covers the rocks in the crust.

magma Melted rock which is found under the earth's surface. When it comes to the surface it may become lava or ash.

mineral A mineral is any substance which is not alive and which can be dug out of the ground.

ore A mineral which contains a useful substance such as a metal.

polished stones Stones which have been made to shine by grinding and rubbing them against rough substances.

precious stones Stones which are rare and beautiful such as rubies and emeralds. They are used in jewellery.

salt A substance found in a mineral called halite. Salt is also found in sea water.

volcano A volcano is a hole in the surface of the earth. It is usually shaped like a mountain. Hot melted rock and gas come out of a volcano.

Index

Photographic credits: Bruce Coleman (Jane Burton) 19, (Keith Gunnar) 20; Eye Ubiquitous 25; FLPA (Hugh Clark) 14-15; Robert Harding Picture Library (G.M. Wilkins) 17; David Paterson 13; Science Photo Library (David Parker) 23; Zefa 5, (H. Schmied) 3, (H. Grondal) 10.